UNDERSTANDING
The Bible

The Story Of The Old Testament

By the same author

UNDERSTANDING
The Bible

The Story Of The Old Testament

by John R.W. Stott

Understanding the Bible

SCRIPTURE UNION

47 Marylebone Lane
London W1M 6AX

Published in the United States by
Regal Books Division, G/L Publications
Glendale, California 91209   U.S.A.

© Copyright John Stott 1978
First published in *Understanding The Bible* 1972
Reprinted 1972, 1973,
Revised 1976
First published in this form 1978

ISBN 0 85421 617 0

U.S. Library of Congress Catalog Card No. 501 7408
ISBN 0 8307 0658 5

Illustrations by Annie Valloton

Printed in Great Britain by
McCorquodale (Newton) Ltd., Newton-le-Willows

PUBLISHER'S PREFACE

UNDERSTANDING THE BIBLE has appeared in several editions, not only in the United Kingdom, North America, Australia and India, but in such languages as German, Swedish, Dutch, Spanish, Faroese, Japanese, Chinese and Thai. The author's objectives set out in his preface are being steadily fulfilled.

Now we are issuing the original publication in five separate volumes in a further attempt to achieve those aims. We anticipate meeting an even wider need; making readily available to new readers the individual subjects on which the Rev. John R. W. Stott has written so clearly.

Their use will not be confined to the individual reader; it will be practicable to use them in study and house groups, etc.

Each book contains recommendations for further reading and an index of scripture references referred to in the text.

PREFACE

Every author owes it to the reading public to explain himself. Why has he thought fit to swell the torrent of books—especially religious books—which pours from the world's printing presses every day? Can he justify his rash enterprise? Let me at least tell you frankly the kind of people I have had in mind while writing. They fall into two categories.

First, the new Christian. With the spread of secularism in our day, an increasing number of people are being added to Christ and His Church who have no religious background whatever. Here, for example, is a young man from a non-Christian family. The Christian instruction he received at school was minimal, and possibly misleading. In any case the fashion was to pay no attention to it. He did not go to Sunday School as a kid, and he has seldom if ever been to church. But now he has found Christ, or rather been found by Him. He is told he must read the Bible daily if he is to grow into spiritual maturity. The Bible is a closed book to him, however—an unexplored, uncharted territory. Who wrote it, he asks, and when, where and why? What is its message? What is the foundation for its claim to be a 'holy' or special book, the book of God? And how is it to be read and interpreted? These are proper questions to ask, and some answer must be given to them before the new Christian can derive maximum benefit from his Bible reading.

Then, secondly, there is the Christian of several years' standing. In the main, he has been a conscientious Bible reader. He has read his portion faithfully every day. But somehow it has become a stale habit. The years have passed, and he himself has changed and matured as a person. Yet he has not developed as a Christian in any comparable way. A sign (and cause) of this is that he still reads the Bible as he did when he was a child, or a new convert. Now he is tired of his superficiality, his immaturity, and not a little ashamed. He longs to become an adult, integrated Christian, who knows and pleases God, fulfils himself in serving others and can commend the gospel in meaningful terms to a lost, bewildered generation.

My desire is to assure such a Christian that the secrets of Christian maturity are ready to be found in Scripture by all who seek them. There is a breadth to God's Word which few of us ever encompass, a depth which we seldom plumb.

In particular, our Christianity is mean because our Christ is mean. We impoverish ourselves by our low and paltry views of Him. Some speak of Him today as if He were a kind of syringe to be carried about in our pocket, so that when we are feeling depressed we can give ourselves a fix and take a trip into fantasy. But Christ cannot be used or manipulated like that. The contemporary Church seems to have little understanding of the greatness of Jesus Christ as lord of creation and lord of the Church, before whom our place is on our faces in the dust. Nor do we seem to see His victory as the New Testament portrays it, with all things under His feet, so that if we are joined to Christ, all things are under our feet as well.

It seems to me that our greatest need today is an enlarged vision of Jesus Christ. We need to see Him as the One in whom alone the fulness of God dwells and in whom alone we can come to fulness of life.[1]

There is only one way to gain clear, true, fresh, lofty views of Christ, and that is through the Bible. The Bible is the prism by which the light of Jesus Christ is broken into its many and beautiful colours. The Bible is the portrait of Jesus Christ. We need to gaze upon Him with such intensity of desire that (by the gracious work of the Holy Spirit) He comes alive to us, meets with us, and fills us with Himself.

In order to apprehend Jesus Christ in His fulness, it is essential to understand the setting within which God offers Him to us. God gave Christ to the world in a specific geographical, historical and theological context. More simply, He sent Him to a particular place (Palestine), at a particular time (the climax of centuries of Jewish history) and within a particular framework of truth (progressively revealed and permanently recorded in the Bible). So the following chapters are concerned with the geography, history, theology, authority and interpretation of the Bible. Their object is to present the setting within which God once revealed and now offers Christ, so that we may the better grasp for ourselves and share with others the glorious fulness of Jesus Christ Himself.

NOTE

1 See Col. 1.19; 2.9, 10

THE STORY OF THE OLD TESTAMENT

Christianity is essentially a historical religion. God's revelation, which Christians cherish and seek to communicate, was not given in a vacuum but in an unfolding historical situation, through a nation called Israel and a person called Jesus Christ. It must never be divorced from its historical context; it can be understood only within it.

This does not mean that the history recorded in the Bible is identical in every respect with the modern view of history. A historian today is supposed to give a full and objective account of all the facts of his period. The

1

Biblical historians, however, made no such claim. On the contrary, they were regarded as 'the former prophets', for they were writing 'sacred history', the story of God's dealings with a particular people, for a particular purpose. They were convinced that God had 'not dealt thus with any other nation'.[1] So their record is more a testimony than a history. They were writing down their own confession of faith.

Therefore, they were selective in their choice of material and (the secular historian would add) unbalanced in their presentation of it. For example, ancient Babylonia, Persia, Egypt, Greece and Rome—each a mighty empire and a rich civilisation—are only included as they impinge on the fortunes of Israel and Judah, two tiny buffer states on the edge of the Arabian desert, which hardly anybody had heard of. The great thinkers of Greece like Aristotle, Socrates and Plato are not so much as mentioned, nor are national heroes like Alexander the Great (except obliquely) and Julius Caesar.

Instead, the scriptural record concentrates on men like Abraham, Moses, David, Isaiah and the prophets to whom the word of God came, and on Jesus Christ, God's Word made flesh. For the concern of Scripture is not with the wisdom, wealth or might of the world, but with the salvation of God. Biblical history is *Heilsgeschichte*, the story of salvation.

The sweep of this sacred history is magnificent. Although it omits great areas of human civilisation which would feature prominently in any history of the world written by men, yet in principle and from God's point of view it tells the whole story of man from start to finish, from the beginning when 'God created the heavens and the earth' to the end when He will create 'a new heaven and a new earth'.[2]

Christians divide history into B.C. and A.D., before Christ and after Christ, believing that Jesus Christ's coming into the world is the watershed of history. So too it is the life of Jesus Christ which divides the Bible into half, the Old Testament looking forward to His arrival and preparing for it, the New Testament telling the story of His life, death and resurrection and drawing out its implications as they began to emerge in the infant church and will one day reach fruition.

In this book I shall attempt to give an outline of the story of the Old Testament. This outline is continued in Book 3 which covers the New Testament story.

The Old Testament is a library of thirty-nine books. The order in which they are placed[3] is dictated neither by the date of their composition, nor even by the date of the subject matter they contain, but by their literary genre. Broadly speaking, there are three types of literature in the Old Testament: history, poetry and prophecy. The historical books (the five from Genesis to Deuteronomy forming the 'Pentateuch' and then twelve more) do tell a continuous story. They begin with the creation of man in Genesis 1 and the call of Abraham in Genesis 12. They go on to tell the story of Israel, the birth of the nation in the rest of the Pentateuch, its varied fortunes during nearly seven centuries in the promised land (in the books of Joshua, Judges, Samuel, Kings and Chronicles), and its rebirth under the leadership of Ezra and Nehemiah. After these seventeen historical books come five books of Hebrew poetry or 'Wisdom'—Job, Psalms, Proverbs, Ecclesiastes and the Song of Solomon—and finally the seventeen prophetical books, five 'major' prophets (Isaiah, Jeremiah, Lamentations, Ezekiel and Daniel) and twelve 'minor' ones (from Hosea to Malachi).

Any reconstruction of the Old Testament story is bound to be somewhat arbitrary. Scholars are still debating, for example, the date of the Exodus and the order in which Ezra and Nehemiah left their Babylonian exile in the 5th century in order to visit Jerusalem. I propose to tell the story according to what I believe is the consensus of most conservative scholars.

The Creation

The Bible begins with a majestic account of the creation of the universe, of earth, of life and of man. It establishes from the outset that the God who later chose to reveal Himself to Israel was not the God of Israel alone. Israel must not regard Yahweh[4] as the Moabites regarded Chemosh and the Ammonites their god Milcom or Molech, almost as a national mascot. For He was no petty godling or tribal deity whose domain and interests were limited to the tribe and its territory, but the God of creation, the Lord of the whole earth.

It is true that the Genesis account of creation is earth-centred and man-centred, in the sense that it is deliberately told from the perspective of man upon earth, but it is above all God-centred in the sense that the whole initiative in the creation lies with the one, true God:

'In the beginning God created . . . and God said . . . and God saw . . . and God called . . . and God blessed . . . and God finished . . .'.

This simple, unadorned narrative, which ascribes wisdom, purpose, power and goodness to the creator God, is far removed from the fantastic and even disgusting creation stories which emanate from the ancient Near East. There are superficial similarities, in that both begin with chaos and end with some kind of cosmos. But the dissimilarities are greater. The Near-Eastern stories are crude, polytheistic, immoral and grotesque; the Biblical account is dignified, monotheistic, ethical and sublime.

The creation story of Genesis 1 begins with God ('in the beginning God created . . .'), continues with progressive stages ('and God said . . .') and ends with man ('so

4

God created man in his own image'). Not many Christians today imagine that the 'days' of creation were intended to be understood as precise periods of twenty-four hours each. Indeed, speaking for myself, I cannot see that at least some forms of the theory of evolution contradict or are contradicted by the Genesis revelation. Scripture reveals religious truths about God, that He created all things by His word, that His creation was 'good', and that His creative programme culminated in man; science suggests that 'evolution' may have been the mode which God employed in creating.[5]

To suggest this tentatively need not in any way detract from man's uniqueness. I myself believe in the historicity of Adam and Eve, as the original couple from whom the human race is descended. I shall give my reasons in chapter 7, when I come to the question of how we are to interpret Scripture. But my acceptance of Adam and Eve as historical is not incompatible with my belief that several forms of pre-Adamic 'hominid' may have existed for thousands of years previously. These hominids began to advance culturally. They made their cave drawings and buried their dead. It is conceivable that God created Adam out of one of them. You may call them *homo erectus*. I think you may even call some of them *homo sapiens*, for these are arbitrary scientific names. But Adam was the first *homo divinus*, if I may coin the phrase, the first man to whom may be given the Biblical designation 'made in the image of God'. Precisely what the divine likeness was, which was stamped upon him, we do not know, for Scripture nowhere tells us. But Scripture seems to suggest that it included rational, moral, social and spiritual faculties which make man unlike all other creatures and like God the creator, and on account of which he was given 'dominion' over the lower creation.

When shall we date Adam, then? The chronology which was added in 1701 to the Authorized Version of the Bible (1611) was calculated by James Ussher, Archbishop of Armagh, from the Biblical genealogies. By working backwards he reckoned that Adam was created in the year 4004 B.C. But the genealogies never claim to be complete. For example, it is written in one of the genealogies of Jesus that Joram 'begat' Uzziah, whereas we know from the Second Book of Kings that he was actually not his father but his great-great-grandfather. Three complete generations have been left out. And recent Near-Eastern studies have confirmed that such omissions were a regular practice in genealogies.

The text itself gives us some better clues. The Biblical account of Adam and his immediate descendants in Genesis 3 and 4 seems to imply a Neolithic civilisation. Adam is said to have been put in a garden to 'till it and keep it'. His sons Cain and Abel are described as having been respectively 'a tiller of the ground' and 'a keeper of sheep', while Cain also 'built a city', which may not have been more than a fairly rudimentary village. These are significant expressions, since farming the land and domesticating animals (as opposed to foraging and hunting), together with primitive community life in villages, did not begin until the late Stone Age. Only a few generations later we read of those who played 'the lyre and pipe' and those who forged 'instruments of bronze and iron'. Since the Neolithic age is usually dated from about 6,000 B.C., this would still suggest a comparatively late date for Adam.

The second chapter of Genesis tells us that work and leisure (six days' work and one day's rest), and monogamous marriage, are 'creation ordinances' instituted by God for man's benefit before sin entered the world. The entry of sin through man's 'fall' or disobedience is described in Genesis 3, and in the following chapters the resulting deterioration of man and his society, and the inevitable judgments of God. The flood seems to have been a comparatively local disaster. It is recorded as an object lesson of God's judgment on human wickedness and of His mercy both towards Noah's family and towards all subsequent generations in His solemn covenant that 'while the earth remains, seedtime and harvest, cold and heat, summer and winter, day and night, shall not cease'.[6] Similarly, the building of the tower of Babel, which may have been a Babylonian *ziggurat*[7] or something similar, is recorded as an example of divine judgment on human pride, leading to the scattering of the nations.[8]

God's Promise to Abraham

It was some time after the year 2,000 B.C. that a new beginning of immense importance took place with God's call of Abraham. It seems to have come to him first in Ur of the Chaldees, then ·in Haran. It summoned him to leave his country and his kindred in exchange for another country and another kindred which God would later give him:

'Now the Lord said to Abram, "Go from your country and your kindred and your father's house to the land that I will show you. And I will make of you a great nation, and I will bless you, and make your name great, so that you will be a blessing. I will bless those who bless you, and him who curses you I will curse; and in you all the families of the earth will be blessed".'[9]

Fundamentally, God's promise was 'I will bless you'. This was spelled out later:

'I will establish My covenant between Me and you . . . to be God to you and to your descendants after you'.[10]

It came to be recognized as the essence of God's covenant with Israel, repeated again and again in the Old Testa-

7

ment 'I will be your God and you shall be My people'. In addition to this covenant-relationship God promised Abraham both a land and a seed. It may truly be said without exaggeration that not only the rest of the Old Testament but the whole of the New Testament are an outworking of these promises of God. In Old Testament days Israel was the promised seed and Canaan the promised land. But the covenant included a reference to 'all the families of the earth' and their blessing. Only now in Christ have these promises begun to be fulfilled. For Jesus Christ and His people are the true seed of Abraham. As Paul wrote to the Galatians:

'If you are Christ's, then you are Abraham's offspring, heirs according to promise'.[11]

The final fulfilment lies beyond history. Then Abraham's seed will be 'a great multitude which no man can number', as many in fact as the stars in the sky and the sand on the seashore, and their inheritance will be the new Jerusalem, 'the city which has foundations, whose builder and maker is God'.[12]

God kept renewing His covenant to Abraham during his lifetime, and then confirmed it to his son Isaac and to his grandson Jacob.[13] The Palestine of their day was in the Bronze Age, but they never settled down to enjoy it. They were nomads. The only territory they possessed was a field near Hebron, which Abraham bought so that he could bury his wife Sarah in its cave.[14]

Jacob (whose other name was 'Israel') had twelve sons. They were, in fact, the original 'children of Israel'. But these progenitors of Israel's twelve tribes all spent their declining years and died not in the promised land of Canaan, but in Egypt, to which famine had driven them. Joseph had become a very senior administrator in Egypt, perhaps even a kind of grand vizier. Such a promotion is not as improbable as some have thought, for the ruling

8

Egyptian dynasty from about 1700 B.C. were the Hyksos, the so-called shepherd-kings, who were themselves Semitic in origin. But Joseph also died in exile, and the Book of Genesis ends with the statement:

> 'they embalmed him, and he was put in a coffin in Egypt'.[15]

When the bald statement is made in Exodus 1.8 that 'there arose a new king over Egypt, who did not know Joseph', one of the succeeding dynasties is meant. This is likely to have been the nineteenth, whose early Pharaohs built the cities Pithom and Raamses, the latter as a royal residence in the Delta area, where the Israelites had settled. It was convenient, therefore, to use Israelite slave labour.[16] And as the years passed, the bondage of the Israelites became crueller and harder to bear, until their lives became 'bitter with hard service, in mortar and brick, and in all kinds of work in the field'.[17]

The Egyptian exile lasted altogether 430 years.[18] What had become of God's promise?

The Exodus from Egypt

As the people of Israel groaned under the Pharaohs' oppressive régime, they cried to God for deliverance:

> 'And God heard their groaning, and God remembered His covenant with Abraham, with Isaac, and with Jacob.'[19]

Indeed, already God was preparing the deliverer He had chosen. By a remarkable providence Moses had actually been brought up in the Egyptian court and learned 'all the wisdom of the Egyptians'.[20] But he had had to flee for his life and was now in hiding in the Sinai peninsula.[21] Here, near Mt. Horeb (or Sinai), where he would later receive the ten commandments for the new-born nation, God spoke to him from the burning bush:

'I am the God of your father, the God of Abraham, the God of Isaac, and the God of Jacob'.[22]

Then God told, Moses that He was about to rescue the people of Israel from their bondage and bring them at last into the land of promise. He further commissioned Moses to go to Pharaoh and demand His people's release.

At first Moses was full of apprehension. He was frightened of Pharaoh, and even more of the response he might get from his fellow-Israelites. But God reassured him:

'Say this to the people of Israel, "The Lord, the God of your fathers, the God of Abraham, the God of Isaac, and the God of Jacob, has sent me to you".'[23]

Moses obeyed. And the people of Israel accepted his leadership. But Pharaoh, probably Rameses II who reigned over Egypt for sixty-six years (1290–1224), demurred. In Biblical language he 'hardened his heart'. Not until the ten plagues had decisively demonstrated Yahweh's superiority over all the gods of Egypt did he finally consent.[24] The date will have been about 1280 B.C.

'The Red Sea' which the escaping Israelites crossed was probably some shallow water north of the northern tip of the Suez Gulf. The miracle lay not in the 'strong east wind' which parted the waters, but in the fact that God sent it at the very moment when 'Moses stretched out his hand over the sea'.[25]

Israel never forgot their safe exodus from Egypt by the supernatural intervention of God. They sang of it in public worship as a signal example of God's power and mercy:

He saved them for His name's sake,
    that He might make known His mighty power.

10

He rebuked the Red Sea, and it became dry;
and He led them through the deep as through a
desert.
So He saved them from the hand of the foe,
and delivered them from the power of the enemy.[26]

O give thanks to the Lord, for He is good,
for His steadfast love endures for ever.
O give thanks to the God of gods,
for His steadfast love endures for ever;
to Him who smote the first-born of Egypt,
for His steadfast love endures for ever;
and brought Israel out from among them,
for His steadfast love endures for ever;
with a strong hand and an outstretched arm,
for His steadfast love endures for ever;
to Him who divided the Red Sea in sunder,
for His steadfast love endures for ever;
and made Israel pass through the midst of it,
for His steadfast love endures for ever.

The escaping Israelites, a large and ragged multitude,
did not travel direct to the promised land along the coastal
route known as 'The Way of the Land of the Philistines'.
They turned south-east to meet their God at Mt. Sinai,
as He had directed Moses. It took them about three
months to get there, and once encamped at the foot of
the mountain they stayed almost a year.

Here God gave Israel three precious gifts—a renewed
covenant, a moral law and atoning sacrifices.

The renewal of the covenant came first. God told
Moses up the mountain to say to Israel:

'You have seen what I did to the Egyptians, and how
I bore you on eagles' wings and brought you to Myself.
Now therefore, if you will obey My voice and keep My
covenant, you shall be My own possession among all

peoples; for all the earth is Mine, and you shall be to Me a kingdom of priests and a holy nation.'[28]

Secondly, God gave Israel a moral law. Obedience to this law was to be Israel's part in the covenant. Its essence was the ten commandments. But these were supplemented both by further 'statutes' ('you shall', 'you shall not') and by 'judgments' which form a body of case-law ('when a man . . .'). The covenant was solemnly ratified by the blood of sacrifice when the people gave a public undertaking to keep God's law.

Thirdly, God made generous provision for breaches of His law. He gave instructions for the building of a 'tabernacle', a rectangular tent measuring about forty-five feet by fifteen, made of dyed linen curtains stretched over a frame and covered with goats' hair and waterproof skins. Inside were two rooms, 'the holy place' and 'the most holy place' or 'holy of holies'. This inner sanctuary was half the size of the bigger room, from which it was separated by a curtain known as 'the veil'. Outside the veil stood a golden lampstand, an incense altar and a table on which baked cakes were displayed. Beyond the veil was the sacred ark, a wooden chest containing the stone tablets on which the ten commandments were inscribed. Its golden lid, called the 'mercy seat', was flanked by cherubim, figures of celestial creatures. In heathen temples these would have formed a kind of throne for the idol. But not in Israel's tabernacle, since the making of idols was forbidden. Instead, God manifested Himself here in a kind of radiance. This was 'the Shekinah', His abiding presence in the midst of His people.[29]

The tabernacle was pitched in a large courtyard. Outside its east-facing door stood a copper basin called the laver, where the priests washed their hands and feet, and the great altar on which the animal sacrifices were burned.

The tabernacle's fabric, furniture and construction are described in Exodus 25–27 and 35–40. The five standard sacrifices are explained in Leviticus 1–7, and full details for the dress, consecration and duties of the priests are given in Exodus 28, 29 and the rest of the Book of Leviticus.

Specially significant is the ritual prescribed for the annual Day of Atonement.[30] The high priest was instructed to take two goats. He was to kill one as a sin offering, to take some of its blood 'within the veil' and sprinkle it on the mercy seat. The blood stood for a life laid down in place of the sinner whose life was forfeit:

'For the life of the flesh is in the blood; and I have given it for you upon the altar to make atonement for your souls; for it is the blood that makes atonement, by reason of the life.'[31]

The veil symbolizing God's inaccessibility to the sinner was to be penetrated on no other day than the Day of Atonement, by no other person than the high priest, and on no other condition than the shedding and the sprinkling of blood. Then:

'Aaron shall lay both his hands on the head of the live goat, confess over him all the iniquities of the people of Israel, and all their transgressions, all their sins; and he shall put them upon the head of the goat, and send him away into the wilderness. . . . The goat shall bear all their iniquities upon him to a solitary land . . .'[32]

These symbolic acts—the shedding and sprinkling of blood, the penetration of the veil and the bearing of sin —all prefigure the atoning work of Jesus Christ our Saviour.

The tabernacle was erected on the first anniversary of the Israelites' escape from Egypt.[33] A fortnight later the Passover was celebrated,[34] and a fortnight later still a census taken of all the men of 20 years or more, who would be fit to fight.[35] The development is striking. Israel is seen first as a disorganized rabble of freed slaves,[36] then as a holy nation in covenant with Yahweh,[37] a 'kingdom of priests' among whom He dwelt, but now (in Numbers) as fighting soldiers, an army encamped in battle array, ready to march to the promised land.

On the twentieth day of the second month of the second year the march began. The tabernacle was dismantled, only seven weeks after it had been erected. The pillar of cloud, symbol of God's guiding presence, began to move, 'and the people of Israel set out by stages from the wilderness of Sinai'.[38]

It must have been an exciting moment. At last, seven centuries after it had been first made to Abraham, God's promise to give His people the land of Canaan was about to be fulfilled. 'We are setting out', they said to one another, 'for the place of which the Lord said "I will give it to you" '.[39]

But their expectation was short-lived. First, the people complained about the shortage of food. Their mouth watered for the fish, the cucumbers, melons, leeks, onions and garlic they had enjoyed in Egypt.[40] Then Miriam and Aaron, Moses' sister and brother, began to undermine his authority.[41] Finally, the twelve scouts whom Moses sent out to reconnoitre the land of Canaan, although the fruit they brought back proved that it was indeed 'a land flowing with milk and honey', added that in their view its inhabitants were invincible:

'The people who dwell in the land are strong, and the

cities are fortified and very large . . . The Amalekites dwell in the land of the Negeb; the Hittites, the Jebusites, and the Amorites, dwell in the hill country; and the Canaanites dwell by the sea, and along the Jordan. . . . We are not able to go up against the people; for they are stronger than we.'[42]

At this report the people wept and wailed. Two of the spies, Caleb and Joshua, pleaded with them not to disobey or disbelieve the Lord or fear the people of the land. But all to no avail. The majority spoke only of stoning them. So God's judgment fell upon His people for their inveterate rebellion. None of that adult generation would enter the land of promise, He said. Only the faithful Caleb and Joshua.

Forty years were now to elapse between the exodus from Egypt and the entry into Canaan, instead of only one or two. Many of them seem to have been spent at the oasis of Kadesh-barnea in the Negeb. But they were years of wandering, too, down south to Sinai again, then north and east through rugged Edomite territory south of the Dead Sea. From here they could have joined the famous 'King's Highway' which ran from the gulf of Aqabah east of the Dead Sea right up into Syria. But the Edomites would not allow them to traverse their territory by this route, so they had to skirt round it farther east.[43] They did not fight the Edomites, for they were kinsmen. But north of them now were the Amorites, also blocking the King's Highway, under Sihon King of Heshbon and Og King of Bashan. Their defeat in battle, and the defeat of the King of Moab's attempts to overthrow Israel, first by hiring Balaam to curse them and then by immoral enticement, are described in Numbers 21–25.

Israel was now encamped on the plains of Moab close to the River Jordan north of where it flows into the Dead Sea. Here Moses gave the people his final charge, preserved in the Book of Deuteronomy. He began by recalling the recent years of tragic wandering and its solemn lessons. He then reminded them of the Lord's covenant and of its conditions. He rehearsed the ten commandments and expounded them in terms of Israel's requirement to love the Lord their God with all their being and to prove their love by their obedience.

'You are a people holy to the Lord your God; the Lord your God has chosen you to be a people for His own possession, out of all the peoples that are on the face of the earth . . . And now, Israel, what does the Lord your God require of you, but to fear the Lord your God, to walk in all His ways, to love Him, to serve the Lord your God with all your heart and with all your soul, and to keep the commandments and statutes of the Lord. . . .?'[44]

Moses went on to expound a number of laws in detail, applying them to the situation the people might expect in the promised land. Two or three times in the course of his exposition he placed before the Israelites the only alternatives:

'Behold, I set before you this day a blessing and a curse: the blessing, if you obey the commandments of the Lord your God . . ., and the curse, if you do not obey the commandments of the Lord your God . . . See, I have set before you this day life and good, death and evil . . .'[45]

The death of Moses is recorded at the end of Deuteronomy. For forty years he had served God and the people of God with extraordinary patience and faithfulness. He had acted as lawgiver, administrator and judge. Above all he was a chosen spokesman of God, a prophet. Indeed the writer adds:

16

'And there has not arisen a prophet since in Israel like Moses, whom the Lord knew face to face.'[46]

Israel's Settlement in Canaan

Already, before his death, Moses by divine command had appointed Joshua to succeed him and to lead the people into the promised land. Now therefore God's word came to Joshua:

'Be strong and of good courage; for you shall cause this people to inherit the land which I swore to their fathers to give them.'[47]

The Israelites were able to cross the river Jordan, as they had crossed the Red Sea, by a supernatural act of God, although this time He seems to have used a land-slide instead of a strong wind to stem the waters for them.[48] Before them stood the ancient walled city of Jericho; its destruction without a siege was their first victory in the land of promise. After an initial defeat at Ai, owing to the disobedience of Achan in stealing loot, the victorious Israelites turned south. They routed a confederate army led by five Amorite kings, and swept on to conquer the southern hill country up to the borders of Philistia.

Next they turned north, where a coalition commanded by Jabin King of Hazor had gathered near Lake Huleh. Although this army was equipped with 'very many horses and chariots', for Israel's settlement in Canaan coincided approximately with the beginning of the Iron Age, it too was decisively defeated:

'So Joshua took all that land, the hill country and all the Negeb and all the land of Goshen and the lowland and the Arabah and the hill country of Israel and its lowland from Mount Halak, that rises toward Seir, as far as Baalgad in the valley of Lebanon below Mount Hermon . . .'[49]

The rest of the Book of Joshua contains a description of the territories which were allocated by lot to the Israelite tribes as their inheritance (chapters 13–22). It ends with a stirring speech which Joshua delivered 'a long time afterward', reminiscent of Moses' charge recorded in Deuteronomy, in which he reminded the people of their history and issued this challenge:

'Now therefore fear the Lord, and serve Him in sincerity and in faithfulness; put away the gods which your fathers served beyond the River, and in Egypt, and serve the Lord. And if you be unwilling to serve the Lord, choose this day whom you will serve, whether the gods your fathers served in the region beyond the River, or the gods of the Amorites in whose land you dwell; but as for me and my house, we will serve the Lord.'[50]

Although the children of Israel were now settled in the land which God had promised to give them, they had not obeyed His command to exterminate its former inhabitants. There is no need for us to be offended by this divine decree. The reason for it can best be described as the need for radical surgery. Canaanite religion was characterized by both idolatry and immorality of the worst kind. The 'baals' were fertility gods, supposed to be responsible for rainfall and harvest, and both ritual prostitution and sexual orgies defiled the 'worship' of the local sanctuaries. So Moses said:

'It is because of the wickedness of these nations that the Lord is driving them out before you.'[51]

Indeed so degraded were the practices of the heathen nations inhabiting Canaan, including the abomination of

18

child sacrifice, that their ejection by Israel is sometimes portrayed in Scripture as the land 'vomiting out its inhabitants'.[52]

Israel's failure to obey God's command resulted in the persistence of heathen culture within her territory and its penetration into her beliefs and practices. This is the situation throughout the period—nearly 200 years—described in the Book of Judges. The same cycle of backsliding, oppression and deliverance kept repeating itself. First the backsliding:

'And the people of Israel did what was evil in the sight of the Lord and served the Baals; and they forsook the Lord, the God of their fathers, who had brought them out of the land of Egypt; they went after other gods, from among the gods of the peoples who were round about them, and bowed down to them; and they provoked the Lord to anger. They forsook the Lord, and served the Baals and the Ashtaroth.'[53]

Then came the judgment in form of a foreign oppression:

'So the anger of the Lord was kindled against Israel, and He gave them over to plunderers, who plundered them; and He sold them into the power of their enemies round about, so that they could no longer withstand their enemies.'[54]

Finally the deliverance:

'Then the Lord raised up judges, who saved them out of the power of those who plundered them.'[55]

But then it happened all over again:

'And yet they did not listen to their judges; for they played the harlot after other gods and bowed down to

19

them; they soon turned aside from the way in which their fathers had walked, who had obeyed the commandments of the Lord, and they did not do so.'[56]

These 'judges' combined several functions. First and foremost they were military leaders, raised up to deliver Israel from her oppressors. Thus Ehud rescued Israel from the Moabites, Deborah from the Canaanites, Gideon from the Midianites, Jephthah from the Amorites and Samson from the Philistines. Next they were spiritual leaders, men of the Spirit, though exhibiting different degrees of devotion to Yahweh. Thirdly, they were judges, as their title indicates, hearing cases referred to them and administering justice in Israel. Nevertheless, there appears to have been but little law and order throughout this period, which is well summed up by the last words of the book:

'Every man did what was right in his own eyes.'

Undoubtedly the greatest of the judges was Samuel. Unlike the others he displayed no military prowess. It was during his term of office that the unthinkable disaster occurred: the Philistines captured the ark of God and transferred it from Shiloh to Ashdod. Samuel relied on spiritual weapons to recover it—prayer and national repentance.

His reputation as a spiritual leader began early. Dedicated to the Lord before his birth, he was brought up at Shiloh under the tutelage of the high priest Eli. Already when he was a young man, we are told, 'all Israel from Dan to Beersheba knew that Samuel was established as a prophet of the Lord'.[57] He acted as a priest as well.

He also judged Israel, going on circuit every year from Ramah, his home town, to Bethel, Gilgal and Mizpah.[58]

However, when he grew old and appointed his sons as judges, they did not walk in their father's ways, but 'took

20

bribes and perverted justice'.[59] So the elders of Israel came to Samuel at Ramah and demanded that he should appoint a king to govern them. As Samuel prayed about their request, it became clear to him that they had rejected not him but God. For Israel had been a theocracy, a nation ruled by God, since its beginning some 250 years before. Therefore Samuel remonstrated with them and warned them that future kings would oppress them. But the people refused to listen and said:

> 'No! but we will have a king over us, that we also may be like all the nations. . . .'[60]

The Establishment of the Monarchy

Israel's first king, Saul the son of Kish, began his reign with great promise. He was rich, tall, handsome, young and popular. He was also a strong patriot, so that when he heard that Jabesh-gilead was being besieged by Nahash the Ammonite he immediately mustered a large army and made a bold dash across the Jordan to rescue them.

He was not so successful against the Philistines, however. They had garrisons on Israelite territory and were a source of constant humiliation to Israel. It was Saul's son Jonathan who one day routed a whole Philistine garrison single-handed, and the youth David (destined to be Saul's successor on the throne) who slew the Philistine giant Goliath. The people were enthusiastic over these daring exploits. But Saul's jealousy was aroused.

The major cause of Saul's downfall was his disobedience. Three times he disobeyed the plain commands of God—in not utterly destroying the Amalekites, in usurping the priestly prerogative of sacrifice and in consulting a medium. God's verdict through Samuel was inevitable:

21

'Because you have rejected the word of the Lord, He has also rejected you from being king'.[61]

Saul fell in battle against the Philistines, together with his three sons, and David was overcome with grief:

'Thy glory, O Israel, is slain upon thy high places!
How are the mighty fallen!'[62]

David had already been designated heir to the throne during Saul's lifetime, but spent the latter years of Saul's reign a fugitive from the king's jealousy. He began his own reign in Hebron, where the men of Judah (his own tribe) anointed him king. But, seven years later, representatives of all the tribes of Israel came to Hebron to do homage to him, and he was anointed king for the second time. He then moved his capital to Jebus (captured only now from the Jebusites), changed its name to Jerusalem, 'city of peace', and brought the ark there from Kiriath-jearim amid tumultuous rejoicing.

David's first achievement was to unify Israel and make the country safe from her enemies. He won victories over all Israel's traditional foes—the Philistines, Edomites, Moabites, Ammonites and Syrians—and ruled over the whole promised land from 'the river of Egypt' (Egypt's frontier wadi) to the River Euphrates. In view of these conquests it was all the more humiliating that he should have to endure rebellion at home, first from his son Absalom and then from a worthless pretender named Sheba.

But David was far from being a war lord. He was artistic, being both a poet and a musician (he had often soothed Saul's melancholia with his lyre). He was also a sensitive spirit, magnanimous to his enemies and loyal to his friends.

Above all, he was devoted to his God. The psalms he wrote express a remarkable depth of spirituality, of penitence after his adultery with Bathsheba[63] and of trust in the God of his salvation. For example:

'The Lord is my rock, and my fortress, and my
      deliverer,
my God, my rock, in whom I take refuge,
my shield and the horn of my salvation,
my stronghold and my refuge,
my saviour; Thou savest me from violence.' . . .

'For who is God, but the Lord?
    And who is a rock, except our God?
This God is my strong refuge, and has made my way
      safe.'

'I love thee, O Lord, my strength.
The Lord is my rock, and my fortress, and my
      deliverer,
my God, my rock, in whom I take refuge,
my shield, and the horn of my salvation, my
      stronghold.

23

I call upon the Lord, who is worthy to be praised,
and I am saved from my enemies. . . .
For who is God, but the Lord,
And who is a rock, except our God?—
the God who girded me with strength, and made my
   way safe.'[64.]

Having built a palace for himself in Jerusalem, David
was anxious also to build a house for the Lord. But
through the prophet Nathan God forbade it, telling him
that his son would be allowed to build the temple.
Meanwhile God added:

'Moreover the Lord declares to you that the Lord will
make you a house . . ., and your house and your
kingdom shall be made sure for ever before Me; your
throne shall be established for ever.'[65]

Israel never forgot God's everlasting covenant with
David. Believers in Israel knew for certain that when
Messiah came, He would be a son of David.

God began to fulfil His promise to David by setting his
son Solomon on the throne, and during his reign the
kingdom of Israel reached the zenith of its magnificence.
It was not for nothing that Jesus referred to 'Solomon in
all his glory'.

King Solomon had a genius for administration and
building. Soon after his accession he prayed that God
would give him wisdom:

'Give Thy servant . . . an understanding mind to govern
thy people, that I may discern between good and
evil . . .'[66]

Solomon's prayer was answered. He divided the country
into twelve regions under twelve officers, whose respon-
sibility was to make provision for the royal household,
one each month of the year. He fortified cities, built up a

standing army, and provided himself with 1,400 chariots and 40,000 horses. He was the father of Israel's navy, whose ships (kept in the Gulf of Aqabah) embarked on adventurous voyages for trade. He built palaces for himself and his queen, halls for assembly, justice and armoury and above all the great Temple, made of hewn stone, cedar and cypress wood and gold. He was also a kind of patron of the arts, and himself the author of numerous songs and proverbs.[67] His reputation for splendour, wisdom and justice spread far and wide, and under his rule his people enjoyed peace and prosperity:

> 'Judah and Israel were as many as the sand by the sea; they ate and drank and were happy . . .
> And Judah and Israel dwelt in safety, from Dan even to Beersheba, every man under his vine and under his fig tree . . .'.[68]

All was not as well as it seemed on the surface, however. Solomon did not love the Lord his God with all his heart. Nor did he love his neighbour as himself. He kept a harem of foreign (heathen) princesses, in defiance of God's prohibition of such intermarriage, and they 'turned away his heart after other gods'.[69] And he was able to maintain his building programme and his grandiose life-style at court only by oppressive measures, including high taxation and a levy of forced labour numbering 30,000 men.

It is not surprising, therefore, that when the people came together to make Rehoboam king in succession to his father Solomon, they said to him:

> 'Your father made our yoke heavy. Now therefore lighten the hard service of your father and his heavy yoke upon us, and we will serve you'.[70]

The old king's counsellors gave Rehoboam wise advice,

which lies at the foundation of every modern constitutional monarchy's ideals of service:

> 'If you will be a servant to this people today and serve them, . . . then they will be your servants for ever'.[71]

But Rehoboam made a rash and foolish mistake. He accepted instead the advice of young and inexperienced counsellors, warned the people that he intended to add to their yoke, and so provoked the ten northern and eastern tribes to proclaim their independence of the dynasty of David.

Saul, David and Solomon had reigned over all Israel for forty years each, so that for the 120 years from approximately 1050–930 B.C. there had been a united kingdom. But now the kingdom was divided. The northern kingdom was Israel, with Jeroboam its first king and its capital city Shechem (later changed to Samaria). The southern kingdom was Judah, with Rehoboam its first king and its capital city Jerusalem. Israel had several changes of dynasty and lasted just over 200 years until the destruction of Samaria in 722 B.C. Judah was more stable, retaining the dynasty of David throughout its longer history of about 350 years until Jerusalem was destroyed in 586 B.C.

The story of the divided monarchy is not easy to follow, as we try to understand the relations between the two kingdoms, their involvement with the mighty empires to their north and south, and the intervention of the prophets who spoke boldly in the name of Yahweh to kings and commoners alike. The Biblical story is further complicated by the fact that much of it is told twice, once in the Books of Kings and once in the Books of Chronicles, the chronicler (? Ezra) writing later with the clear object of emphasizing the importance of the southern kingdom, the Davidic dynasty and the temple

26

cultus. It may be best to concentrate first on the story of Israel.

The Northern Kingdom of Israel

Jeroboam, the first ruler of the northern kingdom, had been one of Solomon's servants. Indeed, so high an opinion did Solomon form of his ability and industry that he put him in charge of a major part of the forced labour levy. Later Solomon had reason to suspect Jeroboam of treason, and Jeroboam fled for his life to Egypt where he was harboured by Shishak (= Sheshonq I of the XXII Dynasty). He only returned after Solomon's death to challenge Rehoboam, as we have seen.

In order to wean the hearts of his subjects from the house of David, Jeroboam was determined to stop them going on pilgrimage to Jerusalem. So he made two alternative sanctuaries, the one up north at Dan and the other down south at Bethel, installed in each a golden calf, and said:

> 'Behold your gods, O Israel, who brought you up out of the land of Egypt'.[72]

It is for this reason that Jeroboam has gone down to posterity as the one 'who made Israel to sin.'

But Judah under Rehoboam was scarcely any better, for alongside the worship of Yahweh the people corrupted themselves with some of the abominations of the Canaanite fertility rituals. Rehoboam had only been king for four or five years when Shishak invaded Jerusalem and denuded the temple of the treasures with which Solomon had enriched it.

Jeroboam was succeeded on the throne of Israel by five kings of whom we know little. But in 881 B.C., some 28 years after Jeroboam's death, the dynasty of Omri began. It was he who established his capital in Samaria,

27

and made it almost impregnable on a well fortified conical hill. But he brought great trouble to Israel by marrying his son Ahab (who soon succeeded him) to the Phoenician princess Jezebel. For she was not only herself a worshipper of Melqart ('Baal' in the Biblical narrative), the main deity of Tyre, but insisted on maintaining at her own expense at court a retinue of 'the prophets of Baal', and involved her husband the king in her idolatrous worship. She also killed the prophets of the Lord.

This brazen apostasy in the palace was the signal for the reawakening of ethical prophecy, which was destined to play a dominant part in Israel and Judah for the next three centuries and more. The first prophet of this noble line was Elijah, who came from Gilead in Transjordan. Austere in his private life-style and fearless in his public ministry, he accused Ahab of troubling Israel by his religious defection. He also challenged the prophets of Baal to a public contest on Mt. Carmel, at the same time taunting the people with double-mindedness, 'limping with two different opinions'.[73] When Baal's prophets had failed to elicit any response from their god, Elijah prayed:

'O Lord, God of Abraham, Isaac and Israel, let it be known this day that Thou art God in Israel, and that I am Thy servant'.[74]

The outcome was an incontrovertible vindication of the living God.

Elijah had a social as well as a religious conscience. He knew that Yahweh was as displeased with the king's oppression of his subjects as with his apostasy. Next to a palace which belonged to Ahab on the plain of Jezreel there was a desirable vineyard owned by a man named Naboth. Ahab coveted it for himself, but Naboth refused to sell his fathers' inheritance. So Jezebel, doubtless with

Ahab's connivance, had Naboth assassinated and proceeded to annex his property. Here Elijah met him:

'Have you killed, and also taken possession? . . . In the place where dogs licked up the blood of Naboth shall dogs lick your own blood'.[75]

Naboth's innocent blood was avenged by Jehu, an Israelite army commander who was now anointed king on the authority of the prophet Elisha. With brutal thoroughness he liquidated the house of Ahab and rid the land of Baal worship.

The dynasty of Jehu lasted nearly a hundred years (c. 841–753 B.C.), almost half the total duration of the northern kingdom. During the early years of the dynasty there was virtually continuous war with Syria, which wrested the whole of Transjordan from Jehu. But it began to be recovered by his grandson, and his great grandson Jeroboam II completed the process.

It was under Jeroboam II (782–753 B.C.) that the northern kingdom of Israel reached its zenith of power:

'He restored the border of Israel from the entrance of Hamath as far as the Sea of the Arabah'.[76]

Peace brought prosperity, prosperity luxury, and luxury licence. True, the local sanctuaries were thronged with pilgrims, and to all appearances Israel was experiencing a religious boom. But the prophets had eyes only for the injustice and immorality of the nation's leaders. Amos, the first great prophet of the 8th century B.C.,[77] was a simple shepherd from the south, but the compulsion of God's word drove him into the northern kingdom to denounce Israel's hypocrisy:

'Thus says the Lord: "For three transgressions of Israel, and for four, I will not revoke the punishment; Because they sell the righteous for silver, and the needy for a pair of shoes—

they that trample the head of the poor into the dust
of the earth, and turn aside the way of the afflicted;
a man and his father go in to the same maiden,
so that My holy name is profaned;
they lay themselves down beside every altar
upon garments taken in pledge;
and in the house of their God they drink
the wine of those who have been fined." '[78]

He knew that religion divorced from morality was an
abomination to Yahweh:

'I hate, I despise your feasts, and I take no delight in
your solemn assemblies.
Even though you offer Me your burnt offerings and
cereal offerings, I will not accept them,
and the peace offerings of your fatted beasts I will not
look upon.
Take away from Me the noise of your songs;
to the melody of your harps I will not listen.
But let justice roll down like waters,
and righteousness like an everflowing stream.'[79]

To Hosea the word of the Lord came through the
agony of his wife's unfaithfulness. For Israel had
similarly broken her marriage covenant with Yahweh
and gone after her 'lovers', the baals of the local shrines.
It was not outward religious devotion God wanted from
Israel, but faithfulness to the covenant:

'I desire steadfast love and not sacrifice, the knowledge
of God, rather than burnt offerings'.[80]

When the dynasty of Jehu came to an end, the northern
kingdom had only about thirty years left. A succession of
military rulers occupied the throne. But the new factor in
international politics was the rise of the great Assyrian
empire. Already in the middle of the previous century

both Ahab and Jehu had paid tribute to King Shalmaneser III. Now the King of Assyria was Tiglath-Pileser III (745–727 B.C.), called Pul in the Biblical narrative, and he embarked on a series of expansionist campaigns. When he reached Israel, he was bought off by King Menahem with a thousand talents of silver.

A few years later (in 735 B.C.) the 'colonel' who was ruling Israel, Pekah the son of Remaliah, entered into an alliance with Rezin King of Syria to throw off the Assyrian yoke. When Ahaz King of Judah refused to join them, they invaded his territory. Ahaz was thrown into a panic, but the prophet Isaiah sought to calm him with a word from God:

'Take heed, be quiet, do not fear, and do not let your heart be faint because of these two smouldering stumps of firebrands . . . If you will not believe, surely you shall not be established'.[81]

Ahaz did not believe. Instead, he appealed to Tiglath-Pileser for help, with devastating results. Syria was overthrown. The Galilean and Transjordanian territories of Israel were depopulated. And Ahaz paid homage to Tiglath-Pileser with silver and gold from the temple, and even to Ashur, Assyria's god.

When Tiglath-Pileser died, Samaria defiantly withheld tribute from Assyria. This reckless act sounded Israel's death knell. The new King Shalmaneser V laid siege to Samaria, which capitulated three years later (probably in 722) to his successor Sargon II. The people of Israel were largely deported, and their country was colonized with Syrians and Babylonians. The resulting mixed population was the origin of the Samaritans.

So the northern kingdom came to an ignominious end. It had lasted just over two centuries. Israel had regarded God's covenant as rendering her immune to His judgment, but the prophet Amos had taught otherwise:

'You only have I known of all the families of the earth; therefore I will punish you for all your iniquities'.[82]

The Southern Kingdom of Judah

So far we have been following the rise and fall of the northern kingdom. The Books of Kings and Chronicles also give some account of the southern kingdom during the same period. But its history was not so colourful, and the names of its earlier kings are not so well known, except perhaps for Jehoshaphat, Ahab's contemporary.

Now, however, the southern kingdom was to continue alone for a further 135 years. Its period of independence was ennobled in particular by two great religious reforms. The first was promoted by King Hezekiah, with the encouragement of the prophets Isaiah and Micah. The second reforming king was Josiah, who was encouraged by his distant cousin the prophet Zephaniah and by the young prophet Jeremiah. .

At the very beginning of his reign Hezekiah repaired and reopened the temple. Then he resolutely removed from his kingdom all the paraphernalia of Assyrian idolatry which his father Ahaz had introduced.

These reforms were certainly the fruit of the faithful witness of Isaiah and Micah who had been denouncing idolatry, empty ritual and social injustice and calling the people to repentance during both the preceding reigns, while Amos and Hosea were proclaiming God's word to the northern kingdom. Here is one of Micah's great oracles:

'With what shall I come before the Lord, and bow myself before God on high?
Shall I come before Him with burnt offerings, with calves a year old?

Will the Lord be pleased with thousands of rams, with ten thousands of rivers of oil?
Shall I give my first-born for my transgression, the fruit of my body for the sin of my soul?"
He has showed you, O man, what is good; and what does the Lord require of you but to do justice, and to love kindness, and to walk humbly with your God?'[83]
Sargon King of Assyria was killed in action in 705 B.C. and succeeded by his son Sennacherib. This seems to have been the signal for Hezekiah's revolt against Assyrian suzerainty. Not until 701 B.C., however, did Sennacherib reach the rebel kingdom of Judah. Having taken its fortified cities, he laid siege to Jerusalem, shutting Hezekiah up (to use his own expression) 'like a bird in a cage'. Fortunately, Hezekiah had taken the precaution of securing the city's water supply by building his famous tunnel from a spring outside the walls to the Pool of Siloam. Even so, the situation appeared desperate. As Isaiah described it:

'The daughter of Zion is left like a booth in a vineyard, like a lodge in a cucumber field, like a besieged city'.[84]

The Assyrian commander taunted the inhabitants of the beleaguered city:

'Do not listen to Hezekiah when he misleads you by saying, "The Lord will deliver us." Has any of the gods of the nations ever delivered his land out of the hand of the King of Assyria? Where are the gods of Hamath and Arpad? Where are the gods of Sepharvaim, Hena, and Ivvah? Have they delivered Samaria out of my hand?'[85]

King Hezekiah consulted Isaiah, and the prophet replied:

'Thus says the Lord: "Do not be afraid because of the

33

words that you have heard, with which the servants of the King of Assyria have reviled Me." '86

The central doctrine of Isaiah's theology was the sovereignty of God. His call to the prophetic office came to him in a vision of the Lord as a king, reigning from an exalted throne. He believed that God was king of the nations and used them as instruments of His own purpose.

So Sennacherib's siege of Jerusalem was lifted. According to the Biblical record 'that night the angel of the Lord went forth, and slew a hundred and eighty-five thousand in the camp of the Assyrians'.[87] It is possible that Herodotus is referring to this incident when he describes a night invasion of the Assyrian camp by field-mice. But he says the mice rendered the soldiers defenceless by eating their bowstrings, quivers and shield-straps, whereas in reality they may rather have been carriers of bubonic plague.

By whatever means it was accomplished, Israel regarded it as an outstanding divine deliverance:

'God is our refuge and strength, a very present help in trouble. . . . "Be still, and know that I am God. I am exalted among the nations, I am exalted in the earth!" The Lord of hosts is with us; the God of Jacob is our refuge.'[88]

The half-century following Hezekiah's death was a time of religious apostasy. His son Manasseh, an abject vassal of Assyria, adopted a policy of religious syncretism and reintroduced the abominations of Canaanite and Assyrian worship which Hezekiah had destroyed. The astral cult, spiritism, Baal-worship and even the horrors of child-sacrifice defiled the land. Amon his son, who reigned only two years, seems to have been no better.

But good King Josiah who reigned from 639 to 609 B.C., turned the scales again and inaugurated even more

34

thoroughgoing reforms than his great grandfather Hezekiah. He ascended the throne of Judah as a boy of eight. When he was still a youth of sixteen, 'he began to seek the God of David his father', which presumably means that he reformed himself and his immediate entourage at court. Four years later 'he began to purge Judah and Jerusalem of the high places, the Asherim, and the graven and the molten images',[89] and the following year Jeremiah received his call to be a prophet.

It was not until five years later still that, as a young man of twenty-six, Josiah led the radical reform of the whole nation. It was the result of the discovery during repairs in the temple of 'the book of the law', which appears to have been some edition or part of the Book of Deuteronomy. The King summoned the people, 'both great and small', to a large public assembly and himself read to them the rediscovered law-book. He then renewed the nation's covenant with God, had all idolatrous objects of Assyrian and Canaanite worship removed from the city and the provinces, closed down the local sanctuaries, prohibited spiritism and human sacrifice, and ordered the Passover to be celebrated in Jerusalem.

> 'Before him there was no king like him, who turned to the Lord with all his heart and with all his soul and with all his might, according to all the law of Moses; nor did any like him arise after him.'[90]

We may be sure that, behind the scenes, Jeremiah was encouraging this reformation. At the same time the prophet deplored what he saw to be its comparative superficiality. He drew the people's attention to the fate of faithless Israel, and added:

> 'Yet for all this her false sister Judah did not return to Me with her whole heart, but in pretence, says the Lord'.[91]

35

Jeremiah often referred to the 'stubbornness' of men's evil heart, 'deceitful above all things and desperately corrupt', and looked forward to the days of the new covenant when God would put His law within men and 'write it upon their hearts'.[92]

In the event Jeremiah was proved right. The results of Josiah's reform did not last, and his son Jehoiakim quickly succeeded in undoing his good work. The new king seems to have used slave labour to build a luxurious palace for himself, and so brought upon his head one of Jeremiah's fiercest denunciations:

'Woe to him who builds his house by unrighteousness, and his upper rooms by injustice; who makes his neighbour serve him for nothing, and does not give him his wages; who says, "I will build myself a great house with spacious upper rooms," and cuts out windows for it, panelling it with cedar, and painting it with vermilion. Do you think you are a king because you compete in cedar? Did not your father eat and drink and do justice and righteousness? Then it was well with him. He judged the cause of the poor and needy; then it was well. Is not this to know Me? says the Lord. But you have eyes and heart only for your dishonest gain, for shedding innocent blood, and for practising oppression and violence.'[93]

Such outspoken talk was not calculated to establish Jeremiah in King Jehoiakim's favour. So when a scroll containing Jeremiah's warnings of the coming judgment upon Judah was read to the king as he sat in his winter house before a brazier, he cut it up with a penknife and threw it bit by bit into the fire.[94] Jeremiah had to go into hiding.

During these years the international scene underwent some important changes. For the past 200 years the Assyrians had been the dominant power in the Near-

East, and the countryside of Israel and Judah had been repeatedly overrun by their armies. But in 616 B.C. Assyria was invaded by Nabopolasser, the founder of the Babylonian dynasty, and in 612 Nineveh (the Assyrian capital) fell after a siege of two and a half months. No tears were shed over her downfall. The Book of Jonah illustrates how reluctantly an Israelite would contemplate Nineveh's repentance and forgiveness, and the prophet Nahum expresses the widespread reaction to Nineveh's oppression:

'Woe to the bloody city, all full of lies and booty—no end to the plunder! ... Behold I am against you, says the Lord of hosts.... All who hear the news of you clap their hands over you. For upon whom has not come your unceasing evil?'[95]

Even after the fall of Nineveh Assyria did not immediately concede defeat. In 609 Pharaoh Necho of Egypt went to her aid, but was himself defeated in 605 by the Babylonians at the Battle of Carchemish on the Euphrates. Now Babylon was supreme, and Judah transferred her homage from Necho to Nebuchadnezzar.

When Nebuchadnezzar's army failed to defeat Necho at the Egyptian border in 601 King Jehoiakim withheld his tribute money. This was tantamount to a rebellion. But Jehoiakim died in 598 before Nebuchadnezzar had had time to quell the revolt, and his son Jehoiachin was left to bear the punitive wrath of Babylon. It fell upon him the following year. Jerusalem was besieged and captured. Three thousand members of the nobility were taken captive to Babylon, and so were the temple treasures. Among the exiles was Ezekiel, who was both a prophet and a priest, and who foretold the departure of God's glory from the temple because of Judah's inveterate sin.

Nebuchadnezzar appointed Zedekiah to the throne of Judah, yet another of King Josiah's sons. He was a weak and indecisive character. His counsellors advised him to look to Egypt for help, but Jeremiah insisted that Judah's only hope of survival was to submit to Babylon. Himself a firm patriot, Jeremiah found it very hard to witness his country's humiliation, and even harder because of his policies to be suspected of treason. His was a voice crying in the wilderness. He stood and suffered alone.

Unfortunately, Zedekiah 'did not humble himself before Jeremiah the prophet, who spoke from the mouth of the Lord'.[96] In 589 B.C. he openly rebelled against Babylon. None of the hoped-for help from Egypt was forthcoming, and Jerusalem had to endure a second siege, this time for eighteen months. The famine conditions were appalling. Jeremiah continued to urge surrender, bringing upon himself first imprisonment and then an attempt on his life.

In 587/6 a breach was made in the walls and the city fell. The city walls were broken into rubble and Solomon's magnificent temple was burned to the ground.

The tiny remnant who were left were put in the charge of Gedaliah, and Jeremiah went on urging them to submit to the authority of Babylon. But Gedaliah was assassinated, and the survivors fled to Egypt, dragging the hapless Jeremiah with them.

The best way to feel Israel's despair when her temple had been destroyed and her people exiled is to read the Book of Lamentations:

'How lonely sits the city that was full of people!
How like a widow has she become, she that was great among the nations!
She that was a princess among the cities has become a vassal. . . .
From the daughter of Zion has departed all her majesty.
Her princes have become like harts that find no pasture;

38

they fled without strength before the pursuer. . . .
"Is it nothing to you, all you who pass by?
Look and see if there is any sorrow like my sorrow
which was brought upon me, which the Lord inflicted
on the day of His fierce anger." '[97]

Yet the godly were not taken by surprise. They knew
that God's covenant with Israel was founded not only on
His promise to be their God but on their undertaking to
obey. From the beginning Moses had warned them of the
consequence of disobedience, and the prophets had gone
on insisting that judgment was inevitable if the nation
did not repent:

'The Lord, the God of their fathers, sent persistently
to them by His messengers, because He had compassion
on His people and on His dwelling place'.[98]

The Restoration from Babylonian Captivity

The Babylonian captivity lasted about fifty years.
Although the exiles had been forcibly deported from their
homes, they seem to have enjoyed considerable freedom.
Jeremiah had written a letter to the first contingent of
exiles, telling them to 'build houses and live in them',
'plant gardens and eat their produce' and 'take wives
and have sons and daughters'.[99]

Their hardest trial was religious, for they felt spiritually
lost in their separation from temple and sacrifice. But
Ezekiel was among them to guide them. He still spoke to
them the word of the Lord. He even claimed to have seen
the glory of the Lord 'among the exiles by the river
Chebar'[100]—the very same glory which had dwelt in the
temple—so God could not after all have entirely aban-
doned them.

In the year 559 B.C. Cyrus II ascended the throne of
the nearby Persian kingdom. Nine years later, by over-

coming the Median army he became King of Media as well, and 'the Medes and Persians' (a familiar expression to readers of the Book of Daniel) became united. But this was only the beginning of Cyrus' brilliant military career. In 546 B.C. he defeated that byword of wealth, Croesus King of Lydia, and all Asia Minor was added to his empire.

The Jewish exiles must have heard of the exploits of Cyrus with growing expectation that their own deliverance from Babylon would not be long delayed. They knew that God was going one day to redeem them, for their prophets had always added visions of hope to their warnings of doom. In these promises of Yahweh the exiles put their trust.

The clearest and most immediate of such promises of salvation are to be found in Isaiah 40–55. There is a debate among Biblical scholars whether these chapters were really written 150 or 200 years previously by Isaiah or came from the pen of some anonymous contemporary prophet. If the authorship is in dispute, however, the message is not. Yahweh is not like the heathen idols. He is the living God, the creator of the world, and He rules in the kingdoms of men. Even heathen rulers are the instruments of His power. It is He who had raised up Cyrus to deliver His people:

'Who stirred up one from the east whom victory meets at every step?
He gives up nations before Him, so that He tramples kings under foot;
He makes them like dust with his sword, like driven stubble with his bow. . . .
Who has performed and done this, calling the generations from the beginning?
I, the Lord, the first, and with the last; I am He.'[101]

Thus says the Lord to His anointed, to Cyrus, whose

right hand I have grasped, to subdue nations before Him and ungird the loins of kings, to open doors before Him that gates may not be closed:

"I will go before you and level the mountains,
I will break in pieces the doors of bronze and cut asunder the bars of iron, . . .
For the sake of My servant Jacob, and Israel My chosen,
I call you by your name, I surname you, though you do not know Me.
I am the Lord, and there is no other, besides Me there is no God;
I gird you, though you do not know Me . . ."'[102]

In the year 539 B.C. the longed-for salvation was given. Belshazzar King of Babylon saw the handwriting on the wall, and that very night Babylon fell into the hands of the Persians. Immediately Cyrus issued two decrees, authorizing the Jewish exiles to return home and to rebuild their temple. The actual text of the second decree, including the materials and measurements of the temple to be built, has been preserved in Ezra 6.3–5. That Cyrus should have issued such an edict is fully consistent with his known policy. As Professor F. F. Bruce has written:

'Cyrus' conception of empire was widely different from Assyria's. The Assyrians imposed the worship of their chief gods on their subjects, and boasted in the subjugation of their subjects' gods. Cyrus . . . had no intention of offending his subjects' religious susceptibilities by such a policy; on the contrary, he would conciliate their susceptibilities by playing the part of a worshipper of their various gods.'[103]

It is hard to imagine the relief, the joy, the exultation of the Jewish exiles when the news of their deliverance reached them:

'When the Lord restored the fortunes of Zion, we were like those who dream. Then our mouth was filled with laughter, and our tongue with shouts of joy; then they said among the nations, "The Lord has done great things for them". The Lord has done great things for us; we are glad.'[104]

Indeed, as the Israelites reflected on their past history and on the steadfast love of their covenant God, they linked together three outstanding examples of His mercy. In each case He took the initiative in His sovereign grace, and in each case He called his people to the land of promise. In the first He brought Abraham from Mesopotamia, in the second the twelve tribes from Egypt, and in the third the exiles from Babylon.

Not that all the exiles took advantage of Cyrus' decree and accepted repatriation. A large number remained. The Book of Esther tells a dramatic story about some of them during the reign of Ahasuerus (Xerxes I), who ruled the Persian empire from 486–465 B.C.

The restoration took place in three clearly defined stages. Not all scholars agree about the order of events, but I give the traditional view. First, Zerubbabel left (538 B.C.) to restore the temple, then Ezra (458 B.C.) to restore the laws and lastly Nehemiah (445 B.C.) to restore the city wall.

The first and main party of Jews left Babylon for home in 538 B.C., a year or so after Cyrus' edict. They were led by Zerubbabel, grandson of King Jehoiachin, and Joshua the high priest. No sooner had they arrived in Jerusalem than they built the altar of burnt offering and laid the foundations of the temple. But then the Samaritans, on being refused the opportunity to collaborate, began to oppose the reconstruction. And the work ceased for about fifteen years.

That it restarted was due largely to the encouragement

of the prophets Haggai and Zechariah. Haggai reproved
the people that they had built their own houses, while the
Lord's house still lay in ruins:

'Who is left among you that saw this house in its
former glory? How do you see it now? Is it not in your
sight as nothing? Yet now take courage, O Zerubbabel,
says the Lord; take courage, O Joshua, son of Jeho-
zadak, the high priest; take courage, all you people of
the land, says the Lord; work, for I am with you, says
the Lord of hosts.'[105]

Zechariah added his word of exhortation:

'The hands of Zerubbabel have laid the foundation of
this house; his hands shall also complete it.'[106]

So the work began again in the year 520 and was
finished in 515, some seventy years after the destruction
of its predecessor.

We now jump nearly seventy-five years in the story to
the second stage in the reconstruction of Israel's national
life after the exile. This was led by Ezra, who was a priest
and a scribe, and (as several scholars have described him)
a kind of 'Secretary of State for Jewish Affairs' in
Babylonia. He was sent to Jerusalem by the Persian King
Artaxerxes I (465–423 B.C.), with royal instructions 'to
make enquiries about Judah and Jerusalem according to
the law of your God'.[107] It was his task to regulate
Israel's religious and moral responsibilities in accordance
with the law.

Thirteen years later came Nehemiah, also sent by King
Artaxerxes, with authority to rebuild the city, and in
particular its walls. On arrival he lost no time, but said
to the local officials:

'You see the trouble we are in, how Jerusalem lies in
ruins with its gates burned. Come, let us build the wall
of Jerusalem, that we may no longer suffer disgrace.'[108]

In spite of opposition and threats the task was accomplished in 52 days. Then a great public assembly was held, at which Ezra and the Levites read God's law aloud and expounded it to the people. There followed a public confession of national sin and a renewal of the covenant to keep God's law in the future. Finally the rebuilt wall was dedicated amid much rejoicing, 'and the joy of Jerusalem was heard afar off'.[109]

Unfortunately, as with previous national reformations, not all the undertakings of the people were kept. For when Nehemiah paid a second visit to Jerusalem a little later, he found several sad irregularities such as a failure to pay tithes, keep the sabbath and avoid intermarriage with the heathen. But Nehemiah dealt faithfully with these matters according to God's law.

It may well be that the prophecy of Malachi belongs to this period, for reference is made in it to identical or very similar malpractices—e.g. mixed marriage and divorce, laxity in the payment of tithes and the offering of blemished sacrifices to God.

The Inter-testamental Period

Israel had to wait another 400 years before her Messiah was born. This is called 'the inter-testamental period', since no book of either the Old or the New Testament was written during it. The voice of prophecy was known to be silent. The author of the First Book of the Maccabees, which belongs to the Apocrypha[110] and describes the events of 175–134 B.C., mentions this several times. He refers to a time of great affliction for Israel as being 'worse than any since the day when prophets ceased to appear among them'[111] and says that Simon was confirmed as leader and high priest in perpetuity 'until a true prophet should appear'.[112]

Nevertheless, there are references to this period in the

44

Book of Daniel, which is certainly one of the most difficult books in the Bible. Questions regarding its authorship, composition and interpretation continue to perplex scholars. It contains several remarkable dreams and visions, some of which are explained, while others are left wholly or partially without explanation.

In general, these predict the rise and fall of the great empires, especially as they affect the people of God. The best-known is Nebuchadnezzar's dream of a vast image or colossus, whose head was made of gold, breast and arms of silver, belly and thighs of bronze, legs of iron and feet of mixed iron and clay. Then (in the dream) a stone hit the feet, and the whole image was smashed to pieces. Daniel interpreted the dream as referring to successive empires. Traditionally, these have been understood as Babylon ('you, O King, . . . are the head of gold'), Medo-Persia (the breast and arms), Greece, the kingdom 'which shall rule over all the earth', and Rome, which became 'a divided kingdom' and did not stand. If this is right, then the stone, 'cut out by no human hand', is the kingdom of the Messiah, of which Daniel says:

'The God of heaven will set up a kingdom which shall never be destroyed . . . It shall stand for ever . . .'[113]

These great empires did follow one another. They provided the setting within which God's drama of redemption was acted out. The Babylonian kingdom lasted from 605 to 539 B.C., the Medo- Persian from 539 to 331, the Greek from 331 to 63, and the Roman from 63 on into the Christian era.

Later chapters of the Book of Daniel are more explicit. His vision recorded in chapter 8 is of a powerful ram, charging west, north and south, with no beast able to stand before it. Being two-horned, it represents the Medo-Persian empire (v. 20). Then 'a he-goat came from the west across the face of the whole earth.' This is 'the

45

King of Greece' (v. 21), that is to say, the rise of the Greek empire under Philip of Macedon. The he-goat from the west 'had a conspicuous horn' between its eyes, with which it struck the ram and broke its two horns. This prominent horn will be Philip's son, Alexander the Great, who, after a series of dashing victories against Asia Minor, Tyre, Gaza and Egypt, defeated the Persian army in 331 B.C.

'Then the he-goat magnified himself exceedingly' (v. 8), referring perhaps to the continuance of Alexander's campaign through Afghanistan as far as India. 'But when he was strong, the great horn was broken', for he died in 323 B.C. in Babylon, and 'instead of it there came up four conspicuous horns', for Alexander's empire was divided into four major regions under his generals— Macedonia and Greece, Thrace or West Asia, Syria and Babylonia (under Seleucus) and Egypt (under Ptolemy).

Of these the last two dominated the fortunes of Israel for the next 300 years. 'They brought untold miseries upon the world'.[114] As in earlier centuries Palestine was a buffer territory between the Assyrian-Babylonian-Persian empires to the north-east and the Egyptian to the south-west, so now Judea was caught between the Seleucids ruling Syria and the Ptolemies ruling Egypt. The former are termed 'the king of the north' in Daniel 11, and the latter 'the king of the south'. Both dynasties lasted until the middle of the first century B.C., and relations between them varied from uneasy co-existence to active hostility and warfare. Judea kept coming under the control now of the one, now of the other.

Returning to Daniel's vision of the he-goat, whose one conspicuous horn had been replaced by 'four conspicuous horns', the vision developed as follows:

'Out of one of them came forth a little horn, which grew exceedingly great toward the south, toward the east, and toward the glorious land. It grew great, even to the host of heaven . . . It magnified itself, even up to the Prince of the host; and the continual burnt offering was taken away from Him, and the place of His sanctuary was overthrown . . . and the truth was cast down to the ground . . .'.[115]

This 'little horn' is interpreted as 'a king of bold countenance' who 'shall cause fearful destruction . . . and shall destroy mighty men and the people of the saints'.[116] He seems without doubt to be Antiochus Epiphanes (175–163 B.C.), who is further designated 'a contemptible person' in Daniel 11.21.

In 167 B.C. Antiochus Epiphanes ordered the suspension of the temple sacrifices, the destruction of the Scriptures, and the discontinuance of circumcision, sabbath observance and the food laws. The climax came in December, when a new altar was dedicated to Zeus, 'the Lord of heaven' (of whom Antiochus claimed to be an incarnation), and unclean animals were offered upon it. Thus the continual burnt offering was taken away and the sanctuary profaned by 'the abomination that makes desolate'.[117]

The king's edict applied to the provinces as well as to Jerusalem, on pain of death. Many complied. Many others resisted, welcoming death rather than defilement. The most fearful tortures and massacres took place, some of which are described in the Books of the Maccabees. The martyrs died 'by sword and flame, by captivity and plunder'.[118] It is probably to them that the author of the Letter to the Hebrews was referring when he wrote:

'Some were tortured, refusing to accept release, that they might rise again to a better life. Others suffered mocking and scourging, and even chains and imprisonment. They were stoned, they were sawn in two, they were killed with the sword . . . of whom the world was not worthy . . .'.[119]

Organized resistance was sparked off by the high priest Mattathias who took it upon himself to kill both a Jewish traitor and the king's officer who was inviting them to sacrifice. This led to a period of guerrilla warfare, in which pagan altars were demolished, Jewish children forcibly circumcised and compromisers slain.

Mattathias died in 166 and was succeeded in turn by three of his sons—Judas who was surnamed Maccabaeus, an epithet meaning probably 'the hammer' or 'the eradicator' (166–161 B.C.), Jonathan (161–143 B.C.) and Simon (143–135 B.C.). The details of their revolt against Gentile rule and of their extraordinary military exploits are recorded in the Books of the Maccabees.

Probably the most triumphant moment in their history came in 164 B.C. when, under the leadership of Judas Maccabaeus, the temple area was purified and the temple itself restored, a new altar was constructed and dedicated, and the sacrifices began to be offered again.

'On the anniversary of the day when the Gentiles had profaned it, on that very day, it was rededicated, with hymns of thanksgiving, to the music of harps and lutes and cymbals'.[120]

The war of independence continued for many years, and political autonomy was not secured until 128 B.C. under John Hyrcanus, Simon's son. He was priest and leader, and some said prophet and king as well. He and his sons annexed a good deal of the territory surrounding Judea.

But in 63 B.C. the Roman general Pompey entered Jerusalem, and penetrated even into the holy of holies, to the horror of the priests. Judea became a Roman protectorate, and Jewish independence was lost again.

48

In 40 B.C. Herod, who had already been military prefect of Galilee and later joint tetrarch of Judea, was made by the Roman senate 'King of the Jews'. Gradually he reconquered his kingdom and in the year 37 B.C. besieged and took Jerusalem, executing Antigonus, the last of the Maccabean priest-rulers. Herod was always unpopular as an Edomite foreigner (although a Jew by religion). Nevertheless he reigned for thirty-three years. It was under his aegis that in 19 B.C. the great reconstruction of the temple began. The work continued almost until A.D. 70, when the temple was again and finally destroyed, this time by the Roman army.

Throughout the uneasy period of Maccabean rule, important movements were taking shape in the Jewish community which later hardened into the various religious parties of our Lord's day.

The revolt of the Maccabees was first and foremost a religious protest, a defiant refusal to compromise with Hellenizing influences. Nothing aroused the indignation of the Maccabees more than the time-serving high-priests, installed by favour of the Seleucid kings. They and their followers are the 'renegade Jews' of the Books of the Maccabees, who wanted even to remove the marks of circumcision and so to ape Greek ways as to wear Greek dress and to build themselves a Greek stadium in which to compete in the games.

The Jews who avoided all contamination from Hellenizing influences were the *Hasidim* or pious ones. They were thoroughgoing separatists, the ancestors of the Pharisees, concerned for religious rather than political freedom.

The Hasmoneans (the Maccabees' family name) were not content with religious freedom; they wanted national independence too. They got involved in all kinds of political intrigue, and their successors were the Sadducees.

The political extremists, wanting to continue the

Maccabean struggle for independence, were the Zealots. They were revolutionary firebrands, determined at all costs to wrest their freedom from Rome.

When, in the fulness of time, Jesus Christ came, the people once tried 'to take Him by force to make Him king'.[121] But He withdrew from them. He had to explain that, although He was indeed a king, His kingdom was 'not of this world'.[122] The freedom He offered was freedom from the tyranny of sin.

'If you continue in My word, you are truly My disciples, and you will know the truth, and the truth will make you free'[123]

The Great Empires

(The dates B.C. are related to each empire's sovereignty as it affected Israel)

854–612	Assyrian
612–605	Egyptian
605–539	Babylonian
539–331	Persian
331–63	Greek (including Seleucids and Ptolemies)
63–	Roman

Some Dates to Remember

c. 1280	The Exodus from Egypt
c. 1050	The Monarchy established under King Saul
c. 1010	King David ascends the throne
c. 930	King Solomon dies. The divided monarchy begins—Israel lasting until 722 and Judah until 586
722	The Fall of Samaria and end of the Northern Kingdom
701	Jerusalem besieged by Sennacherib

50

612 The Fall of Nineveh, Assyria's capital
597 The Fall of Jerusalem. The Babylonian captivity begins
586 Jerusalem is destroyed
539 The Edict of Cyrus. The first exiles return about a year later
515 The restored Temple is opened
458 Ezra arrives in Jerusalem
445 Nehemiah arrives in Jerusalem
323 The Death of Alexander the Great
167 Antiochus Epiphanes profanes the Temple. The Maccabean revolt begins
 63 Pompey reaches Jerusalem; Judea becomes a Roman protectorate

For Further Reading

Israel and the Nations by F. F. Bruce (Paternoster 1963, 254 pages). An authoritative sketch of Israel's history during the 1300 years from the Exodus to the fall of the second temple in A.D. 70. The second half of the book covers the inter-testamental period from the accession of Alexander the Great (336 B.C.). The illustrated edition (1969) includes 36 photographic plates and 3 maps. The author is Rylands professor of Biblical Criticism and Exegesis in the University of Manchester.

Let's Read the Old Testament by Raymond Brown (Victory Press 1971, 187 pages). The Principal of Spurgeon's College has written this simple guide to assist in the reading, understanding and enjoyment of the Old Testament. Each book is introduced and the background, contents and main themes are competently covered.

The Stones and the Scriptures by Edwin M. Yamauchi (Inter-Varsity Press 1973, 192 pages). A well illustrated introduction to biblical archaeology, noting all the principal discoveries that have been made, and drawing out their importance in establishing the reliability of the Bible.

Old Testament Times by R. K. Harrison (IVP 1971, 357 pages). The author's basic conviction is that the Hebrew people cannot be understood in isolation from the whole Near Eastern history and culture to which they belonged. So he traces the history of the O.T. period from the patriarchs to the Maccabees in the light of modern archeological and sociological discoveries. An authoritative work, with over 100 photographic illustrations.

NOTES

1 Ps. 147.20

2 Gen. 1.1; Rev. 21.1, 5

3 The order in which the Old Testament books are placed is different in the Hebrew and the Christian Bibles. The Christian Church followed the arrangement in the Septuagint, the Greek translation made in the 2nd century B.C.

4 Although less familiar than 'Jehovah', this is probably the correct rendering of the Hebrew name YHWH, whose significance was revealed to Moses. See Exodus 3.13–15. It is usually translated 'the LORD' in English versions.

5 I recognize, however, that other Christians who accept and uphold the authority of Scripture reject the theory of evolution as being (in their view) incompatible with Biblical teaching. As the debate continues, it is particularly important for all of us (whichever position we hold) to try to distinguish both between scientific fact and scientific theory, and between what the Bible plainly asserts and what we may like

to think it asserts. I
have more to say on
the whole question of
Biblical interpretation
in chapter 7.
6 Gen. 8.22
7 A temple-tower
    constructed of brick in
    the shape of a terraced
    pyramid and set on an
    artificial mound.
    Ziggurats are known to
    have been built in
    Babylonia as early as
    c. 3000 B.C.
8 Gen. 11.1–9
9 Gen. 12.1–3 RSV
    margin
10 Gen. 17.7
11 Gal. 3.29
12 Rev. 7.9; Gen. 22.17;
    Heb. 11.8–12, 16, 39, 40
13 e.g. to Abraham, Gen.
    15.1–6; 17.1–8; 22.15–
    18; to Isaac, 26.1–5; to
    Jacob, 28.13–15 and
    35.9–12
14 Gen. 23
15 Gen. 50.26
16 Ex. 1 11
17 Ex. 1.14
18 Ex. 12.40, 41
19 Ex. 2.24
20 Ex. 2.1–10
21 Ex. 2.11–15
22 Ex. 3.1–6
23 Ex. 3.15
24 Ex. 4.27–13, 16
25 Ex. 14.21
26 Ps. 106.8–10
27 Ps. 136.1, 2, 10–14

28 Ex. 19.4–6
29 e.g. Ex. 25.8 and 40.34
30 Lev. 16
31 Lev. 17.11
32 Lev. 16.21, 22
33 Ex. 40. 17
34 Num. 9.1–3
35 Num. 1.1 ff
36 Ex. 13.17 ff
37 Ex. 19.1 ff and
    Leviticus
38 Num. 10.11, 12
39 Num. 10.29
40 Num. 11.1–6
41 Num. 12
42 Num. 13.28, 29, 31
43 Num. 20.14 ff
44 Deut. 7.6; 10.12, 13
45 Deut. 11.26, 27; 30.15
46 Deut. 34.10
47 Josh. 1.6
48 Josh. 3.15, 16
49 Josh. 11.16, 17
50 Josh. 24.14, 15
51 Deut. 9.4, 5
52 Lev. 18.24–30
53 Judges 2.11–13
54 Judges 2.14
55 Judges 2.16
56 Judges 2.17
57 1 Sam. 3.20
58 1 Sam. 7.15–17
59 1 Sam. 8.1–3
60 1 Sam. 8.20
61 1 Sam. 15.23
62 2 Sam. 1.19
63 Ps. 51
64 2 Sam. 22.1–3, 32 and
    33 = Ps. 18.1–3 and
    31, 32
65 2 Sam. 7.11, 16

66 1 Kings 3.9
67 1 Kings 4.32–34
68 1 Kings 4.20, 25
69 1 Kings 11.1–8
70 1 Kings 12.4
71 1 Kings 12.7
72 1 Kings 12.28
73 1 Kings 18.21
74 1 Kings 18.36
75 1 Kings 21.19
76 2 Kings 14.25
77 Some, however, would date both Jonah and Joel earlier than Amos.
78 Am. 2.6–8
79 Am. 5.1–24
80 Hos. 6.6
81 Is. 7.4, 9
82 Am. 3.2
83 Mic. 6.6–8
84 Is. 1.8
85 2 Kings 18.32–34
86 2 Kings 19.6 cf. Is. 37.33–35
87 2 Kings 19.35 cf. Is. 37.36
88 Ps. 46.1, 10, 11
89 2 Chron. 34.3
90 2 Kings 23.25
91 Jer. 3.10
92 Jer. 7.24; 17.9; 31.33
93 Jer. 22.13–17
94 Jer. 36.21–23
95 Nahum 3.1, 5a–19b
96 2 Chron. 36.12
97 Lam. 1.1, 6, 12
98 2 Chron. 36.15
99 Jer. 29.5, 6
100 Ezek. 1.1

101 Is. 41.2, 4
102 Is. 45.1, 2, 4, 5
103 *Israel and the Nations* by F. F. Bruce (Paternoster 1963 Illustrated Edition 1969) p. 100
104 Ps. 126.1–3
105 Hag. 2.3, 4
106 Zech. 4.8
107 Ezra. 7.14
108 Neh. 2.17
109 Neh. 12.43
110 The 'Apocrypha' is an expression given to certain books which were not part of the Hebrew canon of the Old Testament. Some contain material which is evidently legendary, and others material which Christians read for ethical rather than doctrinal instruction.
111 1 Macc. 9.27
112 1 Macc. 14.41
113 Dan. 2.44
114 1 Macc. 1.9
115 Dan. 8.9–12
116 Dan. 8.23, 24
117 Dan. 11.31
118 Dan. 11.33
119 Heb. 11.35–38
120 1 Macc. 4.54
121 Jn. 6.15
122 Jn. 18.33–38
123 see Jn. 8.31–36

Your Own Personal Notes

Your Own Personal Notes